The English Gentleman's
Good Fishing Guide

The English Gentleman's Good Fishing Guide

Douglas Sutherland

Illustrated by Alasdair Hilleary

Michael Joseph
LONDON

MICHAEL JOSEPH LTD

Published by the Penguin Group
27 Wrights Lane, London W8 5TZ, England
Viking Penguin Inc., 40 West 23rd Street, New York, New York 10010, USA
Penguin Books Australia Ltd, Ringwood, Victoria, Australia
Penguin Books Canada Ltd, 2801 John Street, Markham, Ontario, Canada L3R 1B4
Penguin Books (NZ) Ltd, 182–190 Wairau Road, Auckland 10, New Zealand

Penguin Books Ltd, Registered Offices: Harmondsworth, Middlesex, England

First published in Great Britain 1990

Typeset in Monophoto 11/13pt Bembo
by Butler & Tanner Ltd
Printed and Bound in Great Britain
by Butler & Tanner Ltd, Frome & London

A CIP catalogue record for this book is available from the British Library

ISBN 0 7181 3314 5

To my sporting wife Diana

Contents

Introduction

I t is said that there are more people in the British Isles who go fishing on a Saturday afternoon than attend football matches. Applied to a soccer-mad nation like the British this sounds like an impressive statistic. In fact, as tends to be a habit with statistics, it does not mean very much. It all depends on what you mean by fishing.

All fishing for sport in or around the shores of Britain can either be in salt water or in what passes nowadays for fresh water. This book is about freshwater fishing and this again is divided into two main codes. There is fishing for what are described as game fish and for what are described as coarse fish and the distance between the two codes is rather greater than that between Moscow and Vladivostok and the atmosphere almost equally chilly.

It is the generally held belief of the more socially sensitive that game fishing is the only form of sport in which a *gentleman* can properly indulge. Because this modest manual is titled *The English Gentleman's Good Fishing Guide*, the perspicacious reader might assume that it is written mainly for those who wish for advice on the pursuit of *salmonidae*, as game fish are generically known and, by and large, the perspicacious reader would be right – but possibly for the wrong reasons.

Isaac Walton whose epic work, *The Compleat Angler*, compendiously describes the method of capture of almost every fish which swims in our native waters from the humblest to the most lordly, was a fervent believer in the democracy of the river bank. All men, in the view of the seer, should automatically be bound together in harmony as Brothers of the Angle to fish side by side in perfect felicity.

If this amity ever existed in anything other than Isaac Walton's imagination it has certainly evaporated in the social climate in which we live today. Many coarse fishing addicts think of game fishermen as a bunch of rich, smell-under-the-nose snobs, whilst there are some of those who have taken up game fishing who regard coarse fishermen as, not to put too fine a point on it, rather coarse.

In addressing this book to the English gentleman, I am conscious that it is not a description ever taken too seriously by the longer-standing members of the breed but it is my earnest desire that those who might take up game fishing for the purpose of improving their social image will not be above benefiting from such behavioural hints as they might find in the pages which follow. Such is the mystique which has grown up in recent years round the sport that fishing, like fox hunting or game shooting, has become very much a matter of dressing the part and comporting oneself correctly in the company of one's fellows if one wishes to be fully accepted as one of their number.

The object of this book is to try to help the reader in not getting his *or her* lines into the most fearful tangle for, when it comes to fishing, the female of the species is, much to the chagrin of the more chauvinistic males, often the more deadly performer of the two.

It is also my hope that this modest offering will not be regarded as being either sexist or racist or whatever else one is required nowadays to avoid being.

Douglas Sutherland
Summer 1990

1

First Pick your Fish

*D*octor Johnson is frequently quoted as remarking, 'Fishing I can only compare to a stick or string, with a worm at one end and a fool at the other'. Actually there is no record that the ponderous Doctor, although not averse to spouting rubbish just for the hell of it, ever perpetrated this particular piece of nonsense.

It is attributed to him by Peter Hawker who, in his work *Instructions to Young Sportsmen*, quotes Johnson as conceding that 'Fly fishing is a very pleasant amusement' and reserving his scorn for fools who indulge in 'angling or float fishing'. This, of course, is quite a different matter and likely to be pure invention by Hawker for whom the word 'sportsman' in a class-conscious, newly-rich Victorian society was synonymous with the word 'gentleman'. Maybe that was how the whole *canard* came about in the first place. The Victorians were masters of invention when it came to splitting social hairs.

As for early records of ladies, as opposed to gentlemen, getting in on the act we have the redoubtable and devout Dame Juliana Berners, Prioress of St Albans who, by her own account, seems to have devoted most of her life to devising new and ingenious methods of catching fish, both game and coarse. Her book *Treatyse of Fishing with an Angle*, published in 1496, remains a classic to this day.

There are, of course, just about as many acceptable ways of catching a fish as there are of killing a cat. Even in the best fishing circles only dynamite and cyanide poisoning are universally considered as outside the pale as engines of destruction and many and wonderful are the devices on the market today calculated to give the hunter as unfair an advantage as possible over the hunted – or, better still, the chap fishing next door to him. Some of these will be discussed in a later chapter.

The most important thing to occupy the mind of anyone adventuring for the first time to cast his or her bait upon the water is to identify and then swot up something on the habits of the fish it is hoped to deceive into attaching itself to the hook. There are, in fact, only two main species with which the fishermen in British waters need concern himself. They are the Atlantic salmon and the trout. Trout come in three distinct and readily distinguishable species – brown, rainbow and sea trout.

Because the salmon is held to be by far the most prestigious to catch both on account of its size and the cost per pound of getting it served up on the dining room table, we will give it pride of place.

The Atlantic Salmon

There have been more books written about the salmon than probably any other single species of fish in the world. There are books on where to find it, how to catch it, how to cook it and what it does with itself when it is not being caught; there are reminiscences and memoirs by the score and enough stuffed fish in glass cases, gazing down in glassy-eyed reproach from the walls of ancestral homes up and down the country to stock a fair-sized fish farm.

For the purposes of this book, however, and the instruction of the embryo angler, all that is really necessary at the outset is to have a good working knowledge of its sex life. It is only when the salmon get the urge to reproduce and leave the comparative safety of their natural habitat in the depths of the Atlantic Ocean that they lay themselves open to capture by the legions lining the river banks, determined to frustrate them in their natural desire to procreate. This is what conservation of the salmon is all about – making sure that there are enough to run the gauntlet with sufficient survivors to ensure ample stocks in the years to come.

Some of the less patriotic salmon try swimming up the rivers of countries like Iceland and Norway but the British have long been wise to this dodge and travel there at great personal cost to be ready and waiting for them, rather after the fashion of football supporters attending an away game.

When the cock and hen salmon manage to achieve the happy event, an act known as spawning, they at once lose any further interest in their eggs and, all passion spent, make haste to return to the depths whence they came. Very few of them make it. So exhausting is the act of procreation – or possibly the effort involved in avoiding being caught on their way to fulfilling their destiny – that they lose their silver magnificence and become hollow-eyed, emaciated and an unhealthy shade of red. These are known as 'spent' fish or *kelts*. To catch a kelt and then not to return it at once, as gently as possible to the water, is one of the gravest sins a fisherman can commit.

It is one of the more irritating characteristics of the salmon that, whereas on their way upstream to spawn they are as fussy and capricious as any prima donna, on their way back to the sea they are apt to attack anything in sight with a gusto which is positively vulgar. Moreover, easy as they are to catch, some recover sufficiently in vigour to put up a sturdy fight when hooked and even look something like their former selves when brought to the bank. The identification of kelts is not always easy.

Be warned! The fisherman who returns to the fishing hut proudly bearing a kelt as proof of his skill will be a figure of fun amongst the more knowledgeable of his companions and risks being mocked without mercy.

The most certain way of identifying a 'well-mended' kelt is by examination of its spawning vent which should, in a healthy fish, be completely closed. If still in doubt, cut a small section of flesh close to the tail with a sharp knife and, if it is tinged with red, return it to the water without more ado.

There is some doubt whether in fact a well-mended kelt, cooked and served, presents, like so much else nowadays, a health hazard. In a recent case a rascally poacher who was before the Bench for selling kelts to unsuspecting housewives on their doorsteps, pleaded in mitigation that he was most careful to sell 'only the very best parts'. The magistrates were unimpressed.

In another case when an evidently more sensitive salesman engaged in the same business was asked by a friend how things were going he replied in his broad Scottish accent, 'Weel, I just sold a rare piece o' fush to a hoose doon the road but when I went back yestreen a' the blinds were drawn so I didna hae the hairrt to offer them anither wee bit!'

Before leaving this brief study of the salmon and its life-cycle, it may be of general interest to chronicle its development from the egg to fully-fledged game fish, if only to familiarize the student with the correct terminology without a knowledge of which it would be unwise to venture into discussion with his fellow sportsmen if he wishes to hold his own in the fishing hut or the smoking room of his club.

When such eggs as survive their natural enemies hatch into tiny fish they only hang about until they become about a finger's length in size before they set out to catch up with their irresponsible parents and start on the long journey down to the sea. At this stage they are known as *parr* and are very much like baby trout in appearance and colouring.

As they grow bigger and get nearer to the sea they begin to take on the typical bluey-black backs and silvery flanks of the adult fish and become known as *smolts*.

After they enter salt water they are faced with taking the first major decision of their lives. Some choose to emigrate far out into the Atlantic, almost to the shores of Newfoundland in some cases, where they may remain for several years before they get the urge to return. Others, less adventurously, hang around close inshore feeding furiously – so furiously that in the course of a year they grow to between three and seven pounds in weight. Then the following spring they return up the river whence they came when they are known as *grilse*. There are those who claim, probably rightly, that pound for pound they are the gamest of all salmon when hooked. Certainly they are the finest of all for the table.

All salmon heading upstream are described as 'running' fish and the more recently they have left the sea, the greater the pride of the fisherperson who catches them. 'Still covered in sea-lice' is the proud description of a fish really fresh from the sea and the description is true enough. Why, for no apparent reason, fresh-run salmon seem to spend a great deal of energy leaping out of the water is not from a general feeling of *joie de vivre* but to rid themselves of the sea-lice clinging to their bodies and which start to irritate them once they get into fresh water. That a salmon should happen to leap out of the water just as the fisherman's fly is passing over its head, often described as the fisherman 'taking short', is very often pure coincidence and no contempt of the fisherman's efforts intended.

The time it takes for a salmon to run the length of its chosen river varies greatly and depends largely on the state of the water. For example, a fish running up a really big river like the Tay can, when the river is in full flood, do the whole journey of some fifty miles or so in a matter of days. Others, held up by low water or through being generally idle, can take months. A fish which has been in fresh water for a long time completely loses its silvery colour, turning to all the darkest colours of the rainbow. It is variously described as 'tartan' or 'a horrible black beast of a thing' and is considered to be fit only for smoking or to be fed to the cats.

The owners of beats in the lower reaches of salmon rivers observe the vagaries of the weather with particular anxiety. With a lot of spate water coming down due to excessive rain or to snow melting in the hills, a fresh run of salmon can go straight through his stretch of the river leaving him dancing in angry frustration on the bank whilst his neighbours in the reaches above rub their hands with glee. There is often not a great deal of love lost between the owners of neighbouring beats on a big river.

There was a famous occasion, before the last war, when the laird of one of the more celebrated stretches of the Aberdeenshire Dee took matters into his own hands to rectify what he considered to be a poor example of neighbourly relations.

There had been a happy understanding between the tenants on the beats on either side of his and himself that should any of the three be lucky enough to be holding fish whilst the others had none, the lucky one would invite the other two to share his good fortune and vice versa. This arrangement lasted happily for many years until the tenant on the topmost beat died. Although the gentlemanly agreement was carefully explained to the new incumbent, when the time came when all the fish were on his beat, no invitation arrived. Worse, when politely telephoned to ask whether he had forgotten his obligations, the new tenant replied with some force that his ghillie had instructions forcibly to remove anyone who dared to cast a fly on his water without his express permission.

A council of war was quickly held and forces joined with the other equally offended tenant with the result that, with the help of a very large poacher's net, the pool holding all the fish on the upper stretch was dragged and the fish towed down to the bottom beat to start their migration all over again! When the offending tenant turned up bright and early on the river, which the previous evening had been full of happily splashing fish, the cupboard was bare.

Fortunately, by no means all salmon start to run up rivers at the same time. Certain rivers are known for an early run of fish. Some, for no definable reason, have a more prolific run in the autumn. On others, especially the very short rivers usually found in the north of Scotland like the Helmsdale and the Oykel, the salmon congregate off the river mouth waiting for a splash of rain before making a dash up stream. On these rivers, one day the sport will be fast and furious and the next you might as well fish in your bath. Very much a case for the fishing tenant of 'you pays your money and you takes your chance.'

There is the delightful story of the tycoon who had taken an immensely expensive salmon beat and succeeded in catching one salmon only.

'Do you realize that damned fish has cost me over one thousand pounds,' he complained bitterly to his ghillie. 'What have you got to say about that!' The elderly retainer rubbed his jaw contemplatively for some time before remarking conversationally, 'I'm thinking you're lucky you didna catch two!'

Trout

By comparison with the majestic salmon, the various species of trout offer far less complicated if no less challenging problems for the game fisherman. Certainly held highest of all in the affections of anyone brought up from childhood to fish must be the indigenous brown trout, content to spend its whole life in its native stream or pond.

Today, when the opportunities for fishing for those whose destiny is to live in big cities are so often restricted to artificially stocked reservoirs, the simplest pleasures of a day by a stream with a hook and a worm and basket full of brown trout weighing only three or four to the pound to show for it may be hard to appreciate.

For them the brown trout loses out alongside the more glamorous rainbow, imported from the western lakes of North America and now widely bred by fish farms to stock our native waters where they often grow to great size. Although there is some evidence in recent years that rainbow are breeding in some rivers in their wild state, they are by nature, like the salmon, a migratory fish and will escape down to the sea unless forcibly restrained from doing so. Otherwise, apart from growing very much larger, they have most of the characteristics of the brown trout. The sea trout, however, is quite another kettle of fish and certainly in habits, if not genetically, far more akin to the salmon.

The sea trout, like the salmon, also spends the greater part of its life in salt water, returning to fresh water at much the same seasons of the year where, as a game fish, it presents in the opinion of many the greatest sporting challenge of them all.

Fishing for sea trout can be a tough and even dangerous business. Long summer nights often spent wading waist-deep in fast-flowing and treacherous waters is not for the faint-hearted or the dilettante whose idea of a day's trout fishing is gently dapping with a mayfly on a placid mill stream. Sea trout addicts claim that the sudden screech of the reel which signals the start of a stern battle with the gamest of all our game fish is ample reward for the cold feet and numb fingers.

Chaque un à son goût.

2

Getting Equipped

I. THE RIGHT ROD

*J*ust as the shooting man should take the greatest care to make sure that he has the right gun that he can grow to love and cherish, so it is with the fisherman when it comes to choosing his rod.

There is, however, one fundamental difference between the two. Whereas the shooting man, unless he be exceptionally wealthy, can manage with one gun which will last him all his life before being passed down to the next and succeeding generations, a fisherman can usually afford several rods and, if keen, undoubtedly will accumulate quite a number during his lifetime. Indeed some fishermen seem to collect rods like the next man collects postage stamps and will arrive at the riverside with bundles of the things, borne before them rather after the fashion of the ancient Roman magisterial fasces.

Whilst this is something that can be carried much too far, there is a certain amount of justification in that, whereas the sporting gun is suitable for dealing with most eventualities its owner is likely to come up against, there are many different ways of catching a fish and different techniques require different types of rod. And equally, although many a good salmon has been caught on a trout rod, it is as well to use the right rod for the right fish.

The Salmon Rod

There is also the consideration that there are two approved and quite different methods of fishing for salmon.

One is known as spinning and entails the casting of a bait. This requires a short, stiff rod fitted with the appropriate spinning reel and many yards of nylon line.

The other is fishing with the fly which requires a flexible, whippy rod, fitted with the conventional type reel and line. The diehard fly fisherman tends to look down on the man who spins as little more than an artisan mechanic whilst regarding fly fishing as true artistry. Certainly, even the most workmanlike of spinning rods has little about it to engender affection whereas a good fly rod is a thing of beauty and a joy for ever.

Whilst the principle of fly fishing, whether for salmon or trout, is basically the same, there is a variety of techniques in trout fishing such as dry fly, downstream wet or lake and reservoir fishing which call for different types of rod. Salmon rods vary only in length and the materials used in their construction. Earlier in the century they used to be very heavy affairs of great length, sometimes up to eighteen foot and made of a weighty wood like greenheart with reels to match of quite prodigious size and often made of heavy brass. Such rods are now museum pieces and fetch staggering sums if they ever come on the market. They come in the same category as wooden shafted golf clubs and gutty balls and are, of course, quite impracticable when it comes to performing the task for which they were originally intended.

The finest examples of the rod-maker's art were those made of cane, which came into their own in the interwar years and flourished for many years afterwards. The aristocrat was the built-cane rod but the more usual split-cane was also a masterpiece of elegance with its fine bindings and varnishing. Fashion is a fickle thing so that today the man who turns up on the river bank with even the finest of cane rods is apt to have the same effect on the rest of the party as H. M. Bateman's 'Guardsman who Dropped His Rifle'. We live in the age of the carbon salmon rod.

The carbon rod is the latest answer to the fisherman's prayer and for which all manner of magical properties are claimed, not least of which is its magically high price. Whether a salmon rod made of carbon enables the person who wields it to throw a fly just that little bit further or place it with greater accuracy over the nose of a rising fish, I do not know. The only time I ever tried one I got my fly caught in a tree, just the same as I usually do with my old split cane. For the carbon rod, however, it must be said that it is a great deal lighter than those wielded by my generation.

The Trout Rod

Trout rods come in many different disguises. The dry-fly purist will probably prefer a stiffer and shorter rod than the all-purpose trout fisherman whereas the fisherman who does all his fishing in those large, stocked reservoirs, which are becoming increasingly popular, goes in for very big heavy rods in the belief that they give him a greater casting distance and an advantage over the more modestly equipped chap standing next to him on the bank.

In fact, the length of a rod does not have a great deal to do with the distance it can throw a fly nor is it necessarily true that the further a fisherman can throw a fly the more fish he will catch. Those distance fly-casting competitions so beloved by the organisers of game fairs produce some spectacular performances in throwing a fishing line but they are really more of a circus act than of any practical use when it comes to catching fish.

A good practical length for a trout rod is ten foot. Most trout rods are in two or three sections. In theory at least, the fewer the sections the better the balance of the rod. I once knew a man who had a rod which broke down into five sections but this was so that he could carry it down his trouser leg when he went poaching.

Balance is above all else important and particularly in a trout rod, so when it comes to buying a reel it is a wise precaution to get the right reel for the rod – or, of course, vice versa.

II. THE RIGHT LURE

Nobody feels the need to equip himself against every possible eventuality more than the fisherman. The capacity most women have for discovering something they desperately need to complete their wardrobe whenever they pass a dress shop pales in comparison with the fever which seizes the dedicated fisherman let loose in a fishing tackle shop. No radiant bride planning her trousseau could be in a greater state of excitement than a fisherman as the date of his annual fishing holiday draws near.

This springs from a naïve belief that there may be some arcane magical property in a particular lure or piece of equipment which will compensate for any lack of skill. A great number of fishermen suffer from feelings of inadequacy and a great many more from a paranoic determination to catch more fish than the next man. No body of people is more competitive than fishermen. Here are some, it is to be hoped, helpful hints on what and what not to buy.

Flies and Things

The number of different patterns of fishing flies on the market is legion. They vary in colour from the downright dull to the most wildly garish. Some are faithful imitations of a real fly; others bear no resemblance to anything ever hatched. This is particularly true of salmon flies, many of which have splendid names like Thunder and Lightning, Silver Doctor and Hairy Mary. The brilliant colours of some of the more improbable looking salmon flies and the even more improbable lures used by fishermen with spinning reels like silver spoons and imitation prawns are explained by the generally held belief that, whilst trout feed voraciously at times, gorging themselves on a hatch of natural flies, salmon eat nothing at all from the moment they enter fresh water until they finally reach their spawning beds. Incredible though it may seem, this belief is supported by the fact that no salmon when caught on rod and line has been found to have anything in its stomach. The theory is that in taking a lure, the salmon is simply making an irritable grab at something which annoys it.

It does not explain, however, why the most effective, if ungentlemanly, way of catching a salmon is by dangling a juicy worm under its nose nor why certain flies are particularly effective on certain rivers and of little use on others. For example, the Blue Charm on the Aberdeenshire Dee, the Jock Scott on the Tweed or the Dunkeld on the Tay. Whatever the truth of the matter, a wise man is he who, when fishing a salmon river for the first time, gathers as much local lore as he can before adding to his collection.

Fly fishing for trout is a much more predictable matter. When a hatch of flies is on and the trout really 'on the boil' it is worse than useless to try for them with anything other than the nearest approximation you can get to the real thing. Brown trout are extremely colour conscious but that is not to say that they will not rise to anything which does not resemble a natural fly. Colourful flies like the Bloody Butcher or the Alexandra, which have no natural counterpart, should have a place in every fisherman's collection. At the same time it is odd how particular and pernickety trout can be. One of the most successful flies ever tied is the March Brown which has a female version that varies from the male only by a tiny yellow tuft at the tail. Quite often trout show the strongest sexual preferences, ignoring the female and relishing the male or vice versa.

All of which is very odd when one considers that the trout, and indeed all fish, are generally considered to be colour blind.

There are many other factors to be taken into consideration when stocking up with fishing flies. There is, for example, the choice of fishing with a single- or a double-hook fly. This really boils down to a matter of personal preference. There is the school of thought which holds that a double hook gives twice the chance of getting the fish firmly attached and those who claim that a single, properly taken, is the more likely to stay taken and not half-hook the fish so that it pulls out. A much more important consideration is size.

It is undoubted that the size of a fly and, to a lesser extent, a spinner or other device is all-important. Some of the largest salmon have been caught on the tiniest of flies so it is not a case of the bigger the quarry, the larger the lure. The 'right' size for the right fly depends on a number of factors of which the brightness of the sun and the height of the water are probably two of the most important. When stocking up with any fly it is therefore sensible to have it in three sizes – very small, a bit larger and larger still.

There is even some evidence that a fish will fall more easily for an expertly tied fly in preference to a more amateurish effort. Nowadays an increasing number of fishermen have taken up the art of fly-tying and no doubt it is a matter of great satisfaction to them to catch a fish on a fly of their own creation. Such an art has the tying of flies become that an annual national fly-tying championship is now held. Interestingly, the championships are almost invariably won by experts who have never tried to catch a fish in their lives! In support of the amateur school, I might remark that one of the few flies I ever attempted to tie in my life also proved to be one of the most successful. It was a case of dire emergency on the river bank and the main ingredient was a few hairs clipped from the beard of that great actor, the late James Robertson Justice.

These remarks are of necessity only of the most general

nature. There are flies specially dressed for dry-fly fishing where the fly sits (hopefully) on the surface of the water. There are others designed to emulate nymphs rising from the river bed to the surface to hatch. There are certain types of flies, known as tube flies, designed for the new type of reservoir fishing and flies considered to be the most effective for sea trout. One of the most efficient of these I have found to be simply a white feather tied to a large hook.

III. THE RIGHT ACCESSORIES

There is really no way in which an adequately equipped fisherman can avoid looking to some degree like a Christmas tree.

For example, even the most pessimistic of fishermen should always carry a landing net. This, by its nature, is one of the most awkward pieces of equipment it is possible to imagine. For trout fishermen there is the landing net which folds and hangs from some part of the fisherman's anatomy so that, theoretically at least, he has both hands free. In fact, if hung from a belt, it catches on everything conceivable whilst to hang it round the neck is not only to risk strangulation but makes it virtually impossible to bring into operation when required.

The problems of the trout fisherman with his landing net, however, pale into insignificance when compared with those of the salmon fisherman. Any net large enough to land even the most modest-sized salmon requires to be so large as not to be portable at all. In times past he would have used a gaff – a pole with a hook on the end with which to pull out large fish and often known in poaching circles as the 'blacksmith's fly' – now he might need a gadget called a 'tailer' which is a sort of running wire noose to slip over the tail of the fish so as to damage it as little as possible in the event of it proving to be a kelt. He will also carry somewhere about his person an instrument called a 'priest', which is a heavy sort of bludgeon with which to administer the last rites on a large fish.

All this paraphernalia is only required in the event of a fish being hooked and landed. In addition most fisherman insist on carrying with them every conceivable aid to hooking a fish in the first place. These are usually carried in a large fishing basket-cum-canvas bag, the accumulated contents of which soon make the housewife's supermarket trolley after the weekly shop seem very small beer indeed.

The fly fisherman in particular will almost certainly have at least two spare reels, one with a white floating line and the other with a tapered sinking line. There will be the obligatory assortment of fly boxes and books, a circular metal container for casts and smaller boxes for things like split-shot and bits of first-aid kit like sticking plaster and iodine as well as ointment for relieving midge bites and medicine like whisky for relieving sudden thirst. There will also be sundry gadgets like a thing for taking hooks out of fishes' mouths as well as pairs of scissors and several standard issue, Swiss Army compendium knives, which have long replaced Boy Scouts' knives as the perfect gift for the man who has everything.

The salmon fishing boffin will notice that the above listings contain no mention of Devon minnows, spoons, prawn mounts and other essential hardware – not to mention multiplying Abu reels and enough spare nylon line as to stretch from the mouth to the source of the Tweed should their patent reels get in a muddle.

The whole operation of getting kitted out to go fishing nowadays should be regarded in much the same light as equipping combat troops, in our modern technological age, for service in the front line of battle.

IV. THE RIGHT CLOTHES

The most important sartorial consideration when out fishing is what you wear on your feet. Apart from fishing from a boat or off the end of Brighton pier, there are occasions when, at some time or other during the day, you will find it necessary to put your feet in the water and sometimes into very cold water indeed. Your main object, therefore, is to keep your feet both dry and warm.

Of course, modern fishing footwear coming as it does in all sizes from knee height to full waders, which tuck in somewhere under the armpits, are of comparatively recent origin and regarded by an earlier generation as perhaps just a little bit *nouveau*. That great sportsman, William Scrope, in his book *Days and Nights Salmon Fishing on the Tweed*, first published in the middle of the last century, informs us:

> Wading in the water is not only agreeable in itself, but absolutely necessary in some rivers in the North that are destitute of boats; and that you may do this in the best possible style, procure half a dozen pairs of shoes, with large hob-nails at some distance asunder: if they are too close, they will bring your foot to an even surface, and it will glide off a stone or rock, which in deep water may be inconvenient. Cut some holes in the upper-leathers of your shoes, to give the water a free passage out of them

when you are on dry land; not because the fluid is annoying, for we should be wrong to say so, but to prevent the pumping noise you would otherwise make at every step.

Mr Scrope also gives this extremely sound advice:

> Avoid standing on rocking stones, for obvious reasons; and never go in deeper than the fifth button of your waistcoat: even this does not always agree with tender constitutions in frosty weather. As you are likely not to take a just estimate of the cold in the excitement of the sport, should you be of delicate temperament, and wading in the month of February, when it may chance to freeze very hard, pull down your stockings, and examine your legs. Should they be black or even purple, it might, perhaps, be as well to get on dry land; but if they are only rubicund, you may continue to enjoy the water, if it so pleases you.

It must be accepted that today most people prefer to try and keep their feet dry but they should still take the greatest care when buying boots or waders. Under no circumstances, for example, should you ever put your trust in any form of fishing boot which has a rubber sole. Take William Scrope's advice in the matter of hob-nails and preferably with a leather sole. Colour, so far as the fish are concerned, is unimportant. Sloane Ranger green is as good as any. Make sure also that the foot size is large enough to be worn with an extra pair of thick stockings for warmth. Most shops which sell waders also sell suitable linings.

When wading there is always the temptation to get just that foot or two further out. It should be resisted. Freezing water trickling down your legs is one of the more unpleasant sensations. Also waders take an unconscionable time to dry out. Probably the best way is to stuff them with old newspapers.

Wading can be a very tricky and even dangerous business. In difficult water where you cannot see your way it is wise to equip yourself with a wading stick to prod the bottom in front of you. A long-handled landing net can sometimes serve this purpose admirably. Particularly hazardous are the chest-high waders. Should you slip and they fill up with water you can be in very bad trouble.

There was the tragic case of the lady, wading far out on the River Dee when, to her immense confusion, she suddenly recognized the lady wading out from the opposite bank as Her Majesty The Queen. Uninstructed as to the protocol for such occasions, she decided to do a deep curtsey with the result that the waters of the Dee flooded in and she was last seen floating upside down on the way to Aberdeen.

(Well, to be absolutely truthful, that is not strictly accurate. The lady in question did do a curtsey with the most uncomfortable result but happily survived to dine out on the tale. However, many who have become inadvertently waterlogged have not been so lucky.)

With regard to other articles of attire suitable for the river bank, it is only sensible, as fishing generally involves some relatively energetic casting, to ensure that the upper garments should be loose, comfortable and preferably made of decent tweed. Those tight-fitting articles of attire which zip up the front and make the wearer look like an advertisement for Michelin tyres are not really quite the thing. If conditions make an over-garment advisable, make sure it fastens with a zip, press studs or toggles. Trying to do up buttons with freezing fingers is not very practical. For the same reason always wear mittens and never gloves. Note that all articles of attire suitable for the river bank are unisex down to the last trouser button – or press stud as the case may be.

A deerstalker-type tweed hat with a peak in front to keep the sun out of your eyes and another at the back to stop the rain running down the back of your neck is a useful type of headwear. Just a word of warning, however. It is not really done to wear a hat or cap with fishing flies stuck all over it. Leave that to ghillies and boatmen. Gentlemen only get flies stuck in their hats by accident.

3

The Royal Connection

*I*t is the most ardent ambition for anyone engaged in
any activity, be it charitable, commercial or merely
social, to obtain the cachet of establishing a Royal Connection. To none does this apply more pertinently than
to those connected with field sports. Nor is there any
Royal activity (unless it be a suggestion of irregular social
conduct by anyone even remotely connected with the
Royal Family) which is more calculated to excite the
media and raise the national blood pressure than reports
of alleged Royal excesses on the grouse moor, the hunting
field or the river bank.

This evidence of Royal patronage, on the other hand,
is what makes field sports so attractive to the socially
ambitious. It may be encouraging, therefore, for them to
know that the field sport most generally enjoyed by the
greatest number of the Royal family is fishing.

The Royal tradition as anglers is said to go back to
George IV. Certainly he was the first of the Hanoverian
monarchs to visit Scotland, although today this historic
pilgrimage is best remembered for his dramatic appearance at the first levee held at Holyrood Palace in full

Highland dress, worn over bright pink tights designed to keep the Royal legs warm. It is hard to imagine him wading up to his middle in the waters of the Dee but he certainly tried his hand at the game and, it is said, the well-known Coachman fly was designed for him by one of the Royal coachmen.

The skill and devotion to the art by his descendant, George V, is, however, far better documented. A French journalist, writing during the 1914–18 war and anxious to show the British King in a good light in the eyes of his French allies, described his sporting exploits on the river bank as follows; literally translated:

He is an angler of the first force, the King of Britain. Behold him as he sits there motionless under his umbrella, patiently regarding his many-coloured floats. How obstinately he contends with the elements! It is a summer day in Britain, that is to say a day of sleet, fog and tempest. But, what would you? It is as they love it, those who follow the sport.

Presently, the King's float begins to descend. My God! But how he strikes! The hook is implanted in the very bowels of the salmon. The King rises. He spurns aside his footstool. He strides strongly and swiftly towards the rear. In good time the salmon comes to approach himself to the bank. Aha! The King has cast aside his rod. He hurls himself flat on the ground on his victim. They splash and struggle in the icy water. Name of a dog! But it is a 'braw Laddie'!

The ghillie, a kind of outdoor domestic, administers the *coup de grâce* with his pistol. The King cries with a very shrill voice 'Hip, hip, hurrah!' On these red-letter days His

Majesty King George dines on a haggis and a whisky grog.
Like a true Scotsman, he wears only a kilt.

Vive, l'entente cordiale.

Of all the Royal family of this generation, it is said that it is the Queen Mother who is the most keen as well as the most proficient salmon angler, closely followed by Prince Charles, although it is said also that, like his father, The Duke of Edinburgh, he is just as happy, if not more so, with a trout rod in his hand on some remote Highland loch.

Quite apart from the Royal connection, fishing, and in particular salmon fishing, has always been regarded as almost the exclusive prerogative of the aristocratic or the very rich. This was simply because, in the days before the 1939–45 war, all the salmon water was owned, by and large, by the great landowning families who fished the rivers themselves and invited their friends very often because they could not find a tenant.

All that has changed now in our new upwardly-mobile, affluent society with the price of salmon beats fetching astronomical prices whenever they come on the market and the cost of renting a decent stretch of water for a week becoming increasingly within the reach of only the seriously rich.

This has moved fishing a place or two higher up on the hit list of the anti-blue-blood-sports fanatics, busy working out the order of precedence for the tumbrils when the glorious day of the revolution dawns.

4

Ladies First

*I*t has been remarked in the introduction to this book
that there is no sport in which ladies can compete on
more equal terms with men than the gentle art of angling.
There are many who would dispute this view and maintain that, either through divine intervention or the luck
of the devil, women are consistently more successful when
it comes to counting the bag at the end of the day. There
is, of course, no question of this being due to their being
more skilful. It is just a matter of their appearing to be
more equal.

What is indisputable is that the largest salmon ever
caught on rod and line in this country is credited to a
female – an eighteen-year-old girl at that. It was caught
by a Miss Ballantine on the River Tay and it weighed
sixty-four pounds.

By the merest chance, it is only fair to remark, the
second largest salmon officially recorded in these islands
(and the largest ever caught on a fly; the 64-pounder was
caught on a bait) was also landed by a woman, Mrs
'Tiny' Morison, fishing on the Deveron and weighing
61 pounds. 'Tiny' Morison was certainly a very fine

fisherperson but her husband, Captain Alec Morison, was in a class of his own. Yet he never caught a salmon in what the Victorians described as the 'portmanteau' class of over forty pounds.

And, by the way, would you believe that the largest spring fish caught this century, was caught on the River Wye in 1923 by a *Miss* Doreen Davey? For those who insist that this would seem to demonstrate a greater degree of skill amongst fisherwomen than fishermen, I would like to give some further examples which at first sight would not appear to contradict the assertion.

There was a recent occasion when four gentlemen had toiled all morning on the Ballathie beat of the Tay without any success. When they returned disconsolately to the boathouse to be joined by their ladies for a picnic lunch, one of their wives who had never handled a fishing rod before, asked whether she might be taught the intricacies of casting with a spinner. Her husband was using one of those patent reels which require, just before the cast is executed, for a catch to be pressed to allow the line to run out freely before it is checked. This was patiently explained to the lady who, unfortunately, at the moment of making her first cast was so overcome by the excitement of the moment that she forgot this small but important formality. The result was that, instead of soaring out thirty yards or more, her bait splashed into the water a matter of a yard from the end of the rod.

At this evidence of female incompetence, the whole party fell about with laughter which turned to dismay when there was a large splash and a magnificent salmon attached itself to the hook. The dismay turned to something like admiration when the lady proceeded to play the fish with the greatest composure before landing it.

There was another occasion when the fishing party had also taken a break for lunch and one of the ladies who had been fishing all morning, instead of reeling in her line and taking her rod up to the hut like any normal tidy-minded fisherman would do, simply left it lying on the river bank with the line trailing into the water.

Yes, of course! When after a most excellent lunch she went to retrieve her rod she discovered that, in the interim, a salmon had obligingly attached itself to her hook.

The third example of the luck of the ladies on the river bank concerns an occasion when a child's nanny, temporarily relieved of her charges, was invited to try her hand. It had been another blank morning for the rest of the party but she wandered off down the bank, rod in hand, to return quite happily an hour or so later with *three* splendid fish.

I am not at all sure, however, that this particular true story entirely supports the contention that women are uncannily lucky for the nursemaid, when invited to give a repeat performance, was only too pleased to oblige. On the second occasion, however, she returned with only two fish!

5

The Ghillie

*B*y and large dictionary definitions of the word ghillie (or gillie) are woefully inadequate. Webster's gets near enough to it with 'a male attendant or servant to a Scottish Highland chief' alt. 'a fishing and hunting guide' but then lets itself down rather badly by claiming further alternatives to mean either 'a stupid person' or, in dialect, 'a woman of easy virtue'.

For all general purposes the reader of this work in search of a more accurate definition would be wise to accept the ghillie as the most important person in his or her life whilst on his stretch of the river bank and as being in much the same position as that of the captain of an ocean-going liner on which he or she is a paying passenger.

Just as the passenger on a cruise liner would be unwise to claim a more expert knowledge of the course set by the ship's captain, so a fisherman would be unwise, to a point of folly, not to accept such indications a ghillie might give as to the best chance of catching a fish. For the ghillie his stretch of water is his kingdom and the fishing hut his castle.

I can well remember a head ghillie admonish his ducal master on an occasion when the fishing conditions were good and, in his opinion, the guests were lingering too long over the hospitable lunch in the fishing hut.

'Ma Gawd, ma Gawd, the deescipline is a' awa tae hell the day!' he cried. 'Put doon yer whusky yer Grace and the lot of you get doon the watter!'

Without a word the Duke and his guests put down their glasses and set about the business in hand.

In these days when most fishing is on more commercial lines, it is a wise paying guest who takes the time and effort to get on the right side of the ghillie who, technically at least, is his paid servant.

The partiality of ghillies as a breed to the odd dram is proverbial. There is the story of the visitor who hired a boat and a ghillie for a day's fishing on a Highland loch. It turned out that the day was wet and windy. All day long the visitor lashed the water unsuccessfully in the driving rain, keeping his spirits up by repeated recourse to his whisky flask without offering his retainer so much as a sip.

Finally, trying to light a cigarette, he found that his box of matches had become so wet that he could not get one to light.

'Is there no dry place in this damn boat where I can strike a match!' he complained.

'You could try the back of my throat,' the boatman replied drily.

The definition of a ghillie as 'a male attendant or servant to a Highland chief' whilst being accurate enough does nothing to describe the unique nature of the relationship he customarily enjoyed with his master.

In the days when the Highland laird could afford to

fish his own river, his ghillie, during the long fishing season, was his constant companion, mentor and familiar friend to a degree enjoyed by no others in the hierarchy of family retainers. When his master had fishing guests, his ghillie virtually assumed the role of co-host and, after their departure, his opinion of their prowess or, more importantly, their personal qualities was frequently the deciding factor in whether or not they were to be asked again.

It must also be said that a ghillie who is also a teetotaller is a very rare phenomenon indeed. One of the most famous ghillies on the Tweed, a river noted above all rivers for the many fishing 'characters' it has produced, was Robert Kerss who was born in 1779 and spent his whole working life in the service of the Macdougalls of Makerstoun. Known as Auld Rob, his master accorded him the rare honour of having a full-length portrait done of him in oils which hangs at Makerstoun to this day.

Of the many anecdotes about Auld Rob, one will serve to demonstrate the sturdy independence and privileged position enjoyed by many of the breed.

On an occasion when his master could not get down to the river, Rob was deputed to take out a guest in the boat. It was an extremely cold day but the guest enjoyed good sport. Each time he hooked a fish Rob rowed him ashore to land it and on each occasion the gentleman refreshed himself liberally from his flask before getting back into the boat and Rob setting to the oars. This happened on three occasions but on the last one, instead of getting back into the boat, Rob strolled off up the bank, 'Rob, where are you going?' the guest called, to which Rob replied, over his shoulder as he stomped off home, 'Them that drinks by theirsels, can fush by theirsels.' And that was the last the guest saw of him.

By contrast there was another well-known character of quite a different nature, called Leekie, whose dominion was on one of the upper stretches of the Dee, near Balmoral. Perhaps it was the proximity of Royalty but each morning he would arrive for his duties by the river, turned out as resplendently as any guardsman going on parade, his perfectly cut plus-fours immaculately pressed and the toecaps of his boots burnished to a sparkling brilliance. To add to his impressive appearance, he sported a handlebar moustache, oiled and groomed to a standard which would have been the pride of any regimental sergeant-major. Even in the most provoking circumstances he was a model of calm dignity. Under no circumstances would he deign to wear waders yet, should it be necessary for him to enter the water for the purpose of landing a fish or for any other reason, he would cheerfully plunge up to his middle in the most icy of torrents. Whatever the rigours of the previous day, the following morning he would be punctually on parade on the river bank as immaculately turned out as ever.

The late Lord Londonderry had for many years an Irish ghillie, called Billy Flynn. Flynn also never wore waders but for quite a different reason. He had a pathological terror of water and nothing in the world would induce him to put a toe in it! Were his employer or any of his guests to do so he would prophesy imminent disaster and remain resolutely on *terra firma*.

Now, when it is the lot of most ghillies to play nursemaid to a new party of 'rods' each week of the season on rented waters, much of the old-fashioned master and faithful retainer relationship has of necessity gone overboard but he would be a wise guest indeed who, on fishing a water for the first time, sought to establish himself in the eyes of his attendant as his 'good and familiar friend'. To seek his advice and throw yourself at his mercy with a suitable affectation of helplessness is likely to reap rich rewards. The goodwill of a ghillie who knows his business is worth a couple of aces in any game of cards.

6

Big Fish

> *L*ord, give me grace to catch a fish
> So big, that even I,
> When talking of it afterwards,
> Shall have no cause to lie.

So runs a once popular jingle.

The obsession most fishermen have with catching a bigger fish than the next man is inherent and their tendency to exaggerate is deeply embedded in their souls.

In their defence it is only fair to remark that the claim that 'the one that got away' was a real monster may not always be the exaggeration that the unsympathetic audience of the relater of the misfortune almost automatically assume it to be.

There is the sad tale of the dead salmon which was found on the banks of the Wye – a river which, particularly in the 1920s, was noted for the number of large fish caught in its waters. The fish was in such a decomposed state that it was impossible to estimate what its weight had been. However, it was $59\frac{1}{2}$ inches long and had a girth of 33 inches compared to Miss Ballantine's record fish, already mentioned, which was a mere 54 inches long and had a girth of only $28\frac{1}{2}$ inches. The sad, nay tragic, part of this story is that the dead giant had an artificial minnow stuck in its jaws. Perhaps, for his peace of mind, it was just as well that the unlucky fisherman never did know just how big that one which got away really was!

In fact, the world record for an Atlantic salmon caught on rod and line is held by a fish caught in Norway in 1928 by the village postman, fishing the Tana. It weighed 79 pounds/38 ounces and one cannot but be impressed by the forebearance of its captor, a Mr Henriksen, for not tipping the postal scales just a few more ounces to make it up to the round eighty.

Another melancholy story of a really big fish caught on our native Tweed, concerns a monster which was taken from the Hirsel water, one of the most famous stretches of that celebrated salmon river and owned by the Earls of Home. The fish, which was caught in the last century, weighed seventy-four pounds and the circumstances under which it did not find its way into the record books are these.

At the end of a day's fishing when the Earl and his guests had retired from the scene of battle, the young ghillie, Jimmy Scott, thought he might try a cast or two on his own account. It was almost dark when he hooked what was obviously a very big fish indeed. Several times in the gathering dusk he caught a glimpse of the monster's back which he was later to describe as 'a great black sow of a fish'. The battle was long and hard fought but when young Jimmy felt he had his adversary beaten, he conceived the idea of crossing to the far bank, the water being very low, and trying to beach it on a shelving bank of gravel. Having not been employed for very long, he did not know the river sufficiently well to realize that in crossing over he had put a razor-sharp edge of rock between the fish and himself. Inevitably it broke his cast.

Although Jimmy was to remain in the service of successive Earls of Home for another fifty years he was never to make the same mistake again!

The following morning Jimmy Scott was early at the waterside to survey the scene of the previous night's disaster when he caught sight of the underbelly of a fish floating just a few yards downstream. It proved to be his adversary of the night before which, when the cast had broken, had floated near-to-dead with the current and the top fly of the two-fly cast had got firmly hooked into an underwater log.

When Jimmy took his monster prize up to the big house and explained the circumstances of its capture, it had been solemnly added to the total of fish caught the previous day with the simple entry in the remarks column in the game book: 'largest 74 lb.'. The Lord Home of the day did not consider it to be fairly caught.

Although records of big fish caught before the turn of the century were not so meticulously kept as they are today, such modesty was remarkable even for those times.

There may be a measure of truth in the pessimistic claim that, for a variety of reasons, the number of salmon (and indeed all other game fish in the wild) caught grows fewer year by year; there can be little doubt, however, that the number of really large fish caught annually has substantially diminished.

Portmanteau salmon, weighing over forty pounds, were relatively common fifty years ago. They were usually cock fish which had spent several years in the sea and were almost always autumn fish. There is a record on the Lower Scone beat of the Tay in September 1924 of three fish being killed on the same day, on the same fly, weighing forty-two, forty-one and eighteen pounds – a total of 101 pounds. They were caught, it is scarcely necessary to add, by a woman, a Mrs Radclyffe.

Whether there are bigger fish today in our salmon rivers than ever before is a matter for conjecture. Whilst the number of fish caught appears to fluctuate from decade to decade, so, too, does the proportion of large fish. The 1920s, for example, were vintage years for really large fish. So, too, appear to have been the last years of the nineteenth century.

Some of the largest fish for which records exist were either caught in nets or by poachers fishing at night and whose reticence about their triumphs is understandable.

The most exact records of fish caught in nets at the mouth of salmon rivers are those kept by the fisheries in the Tay estuary. Of these the record of a fish of over seventy pounds in the Taymouth nets is the best documented. A chronicler of those times, Mr Frank Buckland, describes the fish in a letter headed 'Monster Salmon from the Tay' in the periodical *Land and Water* of 25 June 1870.

Buckland carefully documents the dimensions of the fish, which he got from the Billingsgate fish merchant who had purchased it. It was, he claimed, 53 inches from nose to tail, had a girth of $31\frac{1}{2}$ inches and turned the scales at an ounce or two over 70 pounds – which allowing for the fact that by the time it reached Billingsgate, it would have been out of the water for some considerable time would make it perhaps up to two pounds heavier when it was caught. It is also recorded that the fishmonger paid £9.00 for it which, at today's prices, must rate as quite a bargain!

P. D. Malloch, who owned the famous fishing tackle shop in Perth and was a great expert in such matters, was later to claim that this fish was in fact caught the following year and that he had not only seen it in Mr Speedie's (the Tay netsman) window but had photographed the fish, which he claimed had lost eleven pounds on its journey to London. Other authorities were to claim different weights for this fish so there might even be some doubt whether more than one seventy-pounder was caught in the nets around this time.

It would be surprising, too, if some rod and line fisherman had not tried to get in on the act. No less a pillar of respectability and witness to truth than the Right Reverend Dr Browne, Bishop of Bristol, weighed in (if that is the right expression) with the claim that this seventy-pound fish was the self same one that he had lost on 'the last but one night of the rod season of 1868' after a battle which had lasted ten and a half hours. The good Bishop claimed that he could positively identify it as the same fish 'by a mark where he had seen the tail hook of the minnow when the fish showed itself, and a peculiarity of the firm of the shoulder' – whatever that might mean.

That very much larger fish were the order of the day at the turn of the century is given substance by P. D. Malloch, writing in 1908. Malloch not only established the fishing tackle shop in Perth which bears his name, but had a financial interest both in the nets and as letting agent for private beats. He also wrote several authoritative books on fishing.

'Fish of between 50 and 60 pounds in weight', he claims, 'are often caught in the nets on the Tay, while a few between 60 pounds and 65 pounds are sometimes captured; but beyond this weight fish are rare. I have noticed in our fish-house as many as forty fish over 40 pounds in weight, all caught in one day in the nets ... the average weight of the heaviest salmon taken with the nets each year in the Tay for fourteen years is 60 pounds two ounces.'

Even allowing for the fact that P. D. Malloch was a tireless propagandist for the superiority of the Tay over all other Scottish rivers, these statistics must be considered as impressive.

The claim to have caught the daddy of all salmon, however, is that of a self-confessed poacher whose name has not been handed down but is known to have been a native of Dunkeld. His account of having caught his leviathan in the tidal estuary waters of the Forth some miles below Stirling could easily be dismissed – or indeed might never have become known – were it not that the story was told first-hand, under promise of immunity from prosecution, to Mr W. L. Calderwood who, at the turn of the century, was Chief Inspector of Scottish Salmon Fisheries and one of the most authoritative and reliable recorders of his time of all matters relating to salmon.

Calderwood got to hear of the salmon through the owner of an Edinburgh fishing tackle shop to whom the poacher, an old soldier who eked out his pension making baskets and fishing creels, from time to time sold his wares. The owner agreed that next time the man came to the shop he would try to persuade him to tell his story to Calderwood who promised to regard it purely as a matter of natural history. When the two men met Calderwood described the poacher as being a quiet and respectful type and not at all of the harum-scarum nature of so many of the fraternity. Calderwood quotes the man thus:

> There were three of us fishing the mouth of the Devon [a tributary of the Forth] with a net, in the month of December [1901] when we caught this fish. It took the three of us to lift it out of the water and it was the ugliest great brute I ever saw. It was quite black on the back and had a large head with a huge hooked jawbone. We had nothing to weigh it with but, of course, we knew that it was a quite exceptional fish, so we took it up to the neighbouring farm and got it weighed on the farmer's scales. We weighed it with great care and the nearest we could make it was 103 pounds 2 ounces.

Calderwood professed to believe the man's story, give or take a pound or two according to the accuracy of the farmer's scales. The story is made all the more credible because the man who confessed to having caught it had no ambition to have his name immortalized in the annals of fame. No attempt had been made at the time to take an outline of the fish and it was immediately cut up and sold. *Sic transit gloria mundi.*

The next largest salmon ever recorded as being netted was one that is reputed to have weighed 84 pounds. It was captured in 1869 by a man named Willie Walker in a sparling net, a few miles above the Tay Bridge. Although no proper cast was made of this fish, far from any desire for anonymity, Willie had its outline roughly cut in wood and displayed above the door of his bothy and, it is said of him, could talk of little else so long as he lived.

That sounds a bit more like the true fisherman.

Other Game Records

To give the impression that it is only those who fish for salmon who have a preoccupation with catching big fish would, of course, be entirely wrong. There is no fisherman in the world who does not dream dreams. In the case of big-game fishermen who talk of giant barracuda and mammoth manta ray, it is often obsessional.

It might also be observed that the devotees of coarse fishing are concerned more than most with the catching of a prize fish and getting their names in the record books. The competitive spirit of the coarse fisherman is strong indeed and they appear to be for ever organizing competitions or championships to prove who is the better man, the better fishing club or, indeed, the better in the field of international competition.

Perhaps of all fishing, trout fishing in its various forms is the least infected by this competitiveness which sometimes verges on professionalism. One of its great appeals is its amateurism and that it is an individual, even solitary sport rather than a team event.

Although there are records of the largest sea, rainbow or brown trout ever caught, they do not somehow grip the imagination the way the catching of a record salmon does. Enormous brown trout, for example, dragged from time to time from some loch or another, are apt to be regarded as something of a freak and bear little relation to the merry little fish on which most dedicated trout fishermen cut their teeth and where a two pound fish is a real monster.

By contrast to the little jingle at the head of this chapter, perhaps for the trout fisherman the following prayer is more appropriate:

Big Fish

God grant that I may live to fish
Until my dying day.
And when it comes to my last cast
I then most humbly pray,
When in the Lord's safe landing net
I'm peacefully asleep,
That in His mercy I be judged
As big enough to keep.

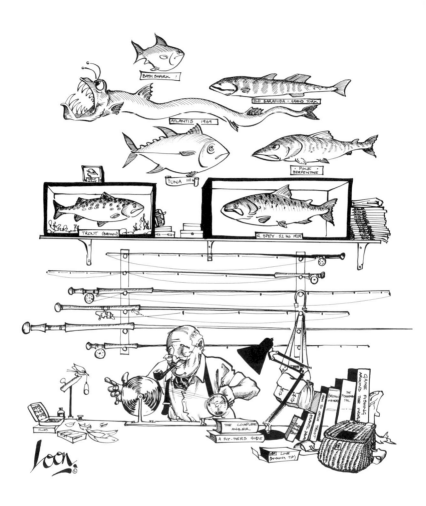

7

The Compleat Angler

N ot many people may know the full title of Isaac
Walton's great classic. It is: *The Compleat Angler or
the Contemplative Man's Recreation. Being a Discourse of
Fish and Fishing. Not unworthy of the perusal of most Anglers.
Simon Peter said, 'I go a fishing:' and they said, 'We also will
go with thee.' John 21.3.*

It is true that this may be on the wordy side for the
modern trend in book publishing but it has the merit of
capturing the interest and directing it to the largest
number of potential readers. Isaac also showed a sound
commercial sense by cutting short the quotation from St
John where he did. It continues: 'They went forth, and
entered into a ship immediately: and that night they
caught nothing.'

One cannot but feel that this would have been counter-
productive in a book which sets out to instruct the reader
in the art of catching fish.

The point of Isaac Walton's work is that, in addressing
himself to the Compleat Angler, he means it in the com-
prehensive sense of the fisherman who is keen, ready and
willing to set himself to the catching of anything from

the most lordly of fish to the most humble; the man who will take pleasure in everything from casting an artificial fly delicately over the nose of a trout to presenting a live frog struggling on a skewer to a predatory pike.

In these days of specialisation and 'high tech' it is doubtful if there is such a being as The Compleat Angler or indeed anyone who has ambitions in that direction. The Great Divide between the aficionados of game fishing and those dedicated to the equally, if not more, skilful arts of coarse fishing, has already been pointed out. There are many widely differing techniques used in the catching of fish in both schools and each have their enthusiastic adherents. It is interesting to examine some of these in so far as they apply to game fishing in these islands.

As has already been observed there are only two approved ways of fishing for salmon; either fly fishing or spinning. Of the two, fly fishing is considered to be by far the more gentlemanly – in addition to being undoubtedly the more skilful. Indeed there are many rivers where, at certain times of the year, only fly fishing is permitted.

There is, too, a certain snobbishness about fishing for salmon from a boat rather than wading from the bank. This particularly applies when fishing from a boat consists simply of trolling a bait out behind the boat and leaving it to the skill of the boatman to position the lure over the most likely places for the salmon to be lying. All that then is required of the fisherman is to stay sufficiently awake as, should a fish give his line a tug, to give it a tug back. This form of salmon fishing is sometimes contemptuously known as 'stockbroker' fishing, perhaps chiefly on account of the fact that you have to be stockbroker-rich to afford it.

When it comes to fishing for trout the options as to methods are considerably more varied. In this context sea trout fishing, regarded by many as the most exhilarating of all forms of game fishing, should be regarded as in a class of its own. The fisherman lucky enough to hook a sea trout in the course of a day's work should regard it as a bonus although there are certain rivers and estuarine waters where the chances are much greater than others.

Trout fishermen tend to be specialists, passionately and single-mindedly devoted to their own form of the art, largely because of the type of water where they have the greatest chance of exercising it. The main division in the ranks of trout fishermen is between those who fish with a dry fly – that is to say an artificial fly which floats on the surface of the water – or a wet fly which is submerged.

Although the dry fly purist is vehement in his view that his form of fishing calls for the very highest degree of artistry and by comparison with which wet fly fishing is child's play, the fact is that it is purely a matter of horses for courses.

The spiritual home of the dry fly fisherman is by the still-running gin-clear waters of an English chalk stream whilst the wet fly man is in his element by the side of a Highland burn where the rushy, boulder-strewn water is the colour of dark brown whisky, flecked with foam and the only habitation in sight is a crofter's butt and ben.

The wet fly fisherman on a chalk stream would be as well fishing in his bath whilst the dry fly purist would be unlikely to keep his fly dry for very long on a Highland burn.

Although dry and wet fly fishing are somewhat different in style and, one is tempted to add, in the temperamental characteristics of their practitioners, they do, by way of variation, share certain similarities.

For example, where a seasonal hatch of mayfly on a chalk stream makes superfluous any other form of inducement to tempt a fish to take, so a sudden hatch of say March Brown on a fast running river will set the wet fly fisherman to rummaging in his fly box to match it. That interesting variation of the dry fly fisherman's art known as 'dapping' which can be so effective on a lovely long warm evening, can also prove deadly when used from a boat on the storm-tossed waters of a loch.

In the same way that example of the fly-tiers' art in simulating a nymph rising to the surface from the river bed to hatch is used in a fishing technique common to both the dry and the wet fly fisherman. Then again they both meet on common ground when it comes to fishing on a loch or lake where conditions of wind and weather dictate which method is likely to be the more successful, and where fishing from a boat over which the fisherman has complete control and is merely a mobile casting platform adds greatly to the pleasure.

It is only of recent years that a new option has opened for the dedicated trout fisherman. This is the creation of new, man-made reservoirs, often, like Rutland Water, of such vast proportions as almost to constitute inland seas and to stock them annually with an equally vast number of trout, both brown and rainbow, and to which flock enthusiastic anglers on high days and holidays, to line the banks in such numbers as almost to stand shoulder to shoulder. A daily ticket entitles the holder to keep a strictly limited number of the fish he catches and weighs in at the end of each session.

This development which is known as 'put-and-take' fishing quite obviously provides a much needed outlet for a great number of fishermen, trapped in an environment which offers no opportunity of pursuing their sport in less artificial surrounds and with fewer restrictions. It is not surprising that under these conditions, new fishing techniques have been developed which in turn call for a modification of traditional equipment and even the devising of new lures to attract the fish whose domestic background seems to have bred in them a sophistication which sets them apart from their more rustic relatives.

One wonders what Isaac Walton and his boon companion of the river bank, Charles Cotton, would have thought of their gentle art in the ever increasing competitiveness in our modern world.

> The river Dove flows down its Dale,
>   And ripples just as sweetly,
> As when good Master Walton hied,
> With Master Cotton by his side,
>   To angle there compleatly.
>
> And sometimes Master Walton scored,
>   And sometimes Master Cotton;
> And sometimes neither caught a fish,
> When Walton sadly murmured 'Pish!'
>   And Cotton muttered 'Rotten!'
>
>   (E. V. Lucas, Izaak and Charles.)

8

Poaching Ways

*T*here has always been a great sympathy amongst country folk for that traditionally colourful country character, the local poacher. In more spacious days it was not unknown for his sworn enemy the gamekeeper to buy him the odd pint in the pub. 'At least I know where the b***** is when he is supping my beer,' as one headkeeper once put it. That he was generally a deplorable fellow with a great capacity for strong liquor and a marked aversion to taking regular gainful employment mattered not in the least and many a respectable citizen envied him the way in which he cocked a snook at society.

I can well remember encountering one of the fraternity in the bar of a small hotel where I was staying on a fishing holiday in the wilds of Connemara. He was a most genial character and we soon fell to discussing the merits and demerits of various local waters. After we had sunk a comradely dram or two, which I strongly suspected had never seen the inside of a bonded warehouse, he enquired with typical Irish courtesy if I might be of a mind to accompany him on a fishing expedition the following evening on a river which he assured me was fairly teeming with the 'beasties'.

It was hardly an invitation I would be likely to refuse, especially coming as it did from one of the obviously well-respected local worthies. As I did not know the nature of the water, however, I thought to enquire of him what I should put on my feet in the way of boots or waders.

'Sorr,' he said, leaning towards me and laying a strong, workmanlike hand on my arm, 'when ye come fishing wi' me, ye wear running shoes!'

It was only then that the penny dropped. I must confess, to my shame, that I went along anyway. It seemed only polite.

Historically, the attitude of the law towards poaching north of the Border has always been an ambivalent one. In England such was the absolute power of the great landowners that the laws they themselves passed to protect their own game were draconian in the extreme. Transportation for life to the colonies was at the lower end of the scale of penalties and public hanging *pour encourager les autres* not at all unusual.

In Scotland the penalties for poaching salmon during the fishing season have never been heavy and to take trout has never been a crime at all. In far off times, however, the penalties for killing salmon in the spawning season, *whether poached or not,* used to be very heavy indeed. This had its origins in the poverty-stricken economy of the country and the recognition by the authorities of the need to preserve a valuable food resource. Thus to take the odd fish unlawfully in the lawful season was of little account compared with taking spawning fish. It was the protection of the fish itself rather than the selfish interests of the landowners with which the law was concerned.

An Act, passed in James I's first Parliament in 1424, declares:

> Quha sa ever be convict of slauchter of Salmons in time forbidden by the law, he sall pay fourtie shillings for the unlaw, and at the third time, gif he be convicted of trespasse, he sall tyne his life ...

Although that the penalty should escalate from forty shillings for a first offender (even allowing for forty shillings, Scots, being in those days an enormous sum of money) to execution for a third offender might seem to be fairly steep, it has always seemed to me to be, in principle, pretty sound.

Since those good old days the penalties for taking salmon, whether spawning or not, have become progressively less onerous until the present when they verge on the trivial. This is particularly unfortunate since the day of the one-for-the-pot taken by the local lovable rascal has long since given way to the escalation of poaching into the realms of very big business indeed, in the hands of highly organized gangs of criminals.

The existence of ruthless gangs of salmon poachers, however, is not so new a phenomenon as might be imagined. Here is an extract from Thomas Stoddart's book *The Tweed and its Tributaries*, written in the middle of the last century and which describes a singularly bloody incident:

> Such a massacre as took place near Melrose in 1846, when upwards of three hundred breeding fish writhed and bled

on a single liester,* and at least six thousand, which had escaped the toils of the Berwick fishermen [the netsmen at the mouth of the river] and formed the hope and stay of future seasons of abundance, along the course of the river! From the effect of this bloody onslaught, the Tweed has not yet recovered.

Although the professional sea-netters and poisoners are regarded with a very proper horror by most law-abiding citizens, it is not an obloquy which is always extended to the less profit-motivated but nonetheless organized defiance of the poaching laws which today is becoming increasingly prevalent. There lingers on, particularly amongst the loonier elements of the left, a feeling that all poaching is simply an expression of the rights of the people against the established bastions of privilege.

One can imagine the feelings of one fishing tenant who had paid a considerable sum of money for a day's salmon fishing for his friends and himself on a beat on the upper reaches of the Tay, when he arrived with his guests to find the river bank already lined with a busload of anglers, spaced every few yards and casting away happily.

They were, it turned out, a party of coal miners from

---

* The liester was a particularly ferocious and effective weapon of the poacher's trade in those days. Sometimes known as a 'waster', it consisted of a five pronged spear with a single barb on each prong which was attached to a long pole. Used on the shallow spawning grounds at the head of a river where the fish are relatively helpless it was a dangerous device indeed.

Today, such are the advances in modern scientific poaching, a very small amount of a preparation called Cymag (cyanide) dropped into the water at the top of a salmon pool, can have much the same effect as a dozen liesters.

a Fifeshire pit who, happening to be on strike at the time and with nothing better to do, had decided to organize an outing. They claimed that they were only fishing for trout and were quite within their rights. When the outraged tenant protested, pointing out that anyway they were all armed with salmon rods, it was made clear to him that any further objections and he and his party would finish up in the river.

A similar incident was related to me by that ardent campaigner for the reform of the poaching laws, the late Lord Biddulph. He was for many years one of the leading members of a syndicate which fished the Grimersta river in North Lewis in the Outer Hebrides, regarded by many as one of our finest salmon rivers. Although the Grimersta itself is a short river only six miles long, it gives access to many of the inland lochs with which the most northerly of the islands of the Outer Hebrides are scattered and which are long renowned for the spectacular run of salmon fresh from their salt water migration on the island's western Atlantic seaboard. It might also be said that North Lewis has more than its fair share of protesters against authority amongst its sparse population.

It happened that one evening around dusk His Lordship was on his own having a few casts from the bank not very far from the fishing lodge when he became aware that he was not alone. Turning his head he could see a man's head, clad in a Balaclava helmet, silhouetted against the skyline.

'Who the devil are you?' he called out.

'F*** off!' came the reply and upon which four more similarly clad heads rose out of the heather.

'Good Heavens!' I exclaimed when he related this story to me. 'What did you do?'

Robert Biddulph shrugged his shoulders.

'I f★★★ed off,' he said. 'What would you have done?'

It is not, however, the citizenry who use excuses of political protest to justify their anti-social activities against whom more realistic legislation is so urgently required but the criminal organizations, equipped with fast boats, feather-light monofil nets and diving gear and wireless sets tuned into the police network to give early warning.

The main battlefield in what amounts to open warfare is no longer the riverbank but inshore off the mouths of the salmon rivers where the fish congregate as they prepare to run the gauntlet of the many other hazards they will have to face before reaching their spawning beds.

It seems indeed a long time since all a poacher felt in need of was a pair of running shoes!

9

Mind Your Manners

*F*ishing is, as most practitioners of the sport would admit, a solitary business almost to the point of being anti-social. Crowd as they may along the banks of a reservoir or crouch, each on his own stool, a bare arm's length apart alongside a canal, there is not one amongst them who would not damn his companions to perdition and wish himself to be the sole monarch of all he surveys.

Get a fisher away from the waterside, however, and he is the most social and clubbable of men. In fact, there are more fishing clubs in various disguises than exist in any other sport. In many areas to belong to a fishing club is far more *comme il faut* than to belong to a tennis club. There are clubs which exist for the sole purpose of holding the rights to fish certain waters and can cost many thousands of pounds to belong to, like the Yorkshire Fly Fishers' Club which has the rights on many of the finest trout waters in the north of England. By contrast there is the Fly Fishers' Club in London which has no water of its own at all and where the sociable and highly convivial members entertain their friends and distinguished guests to a lavish dinner party each year when they play rather

SILENCE!
DO NOT DISTURB
THE FISH

a dirty trick on the principal guest. Not only is he required to make an after-dinner speech but he is presented with all 'the makings' and required to tie a fly. The success of this operation is generally in inverse ratio to the degree in which the victim has partaken of the hospitality.

Nowadays when so much fishing is let for a period of a week or more to parties of rods, fisherpersons often find themselves obliged not only to co-exist on the river bank during the day but to fraternize socially afterwards in small hotels and fishing lodges, which have been taken over for the purpose and where great store is set on the joys of *après-fish*.

This is not always a blinding success as it is hard to imagine, as has already been remarked, any group of people, temporarily bound together only by the common bond of the sport they love who are more individually competitive and imbued with a burning desire to come out top dog. This applies equally to coarse fishermen, each seated patiently on his canvas stool with his Thermos flask and corned beef sandwiches, as the slap-you-on-the-back jolly good fellows who insist on circulating the whisky bottle in the fishing hut. Such is their nature that they will stop at nothing to take an unfair advantage even if it entails making you drunk, whilst being the quickest to take offence if they feel anyone else is trying to put one over on them.

In a fishing party any offence, real or imagined, committed early on in the proceedings is set fair to go forth and multiply so that when the time comes for the bidding of fond farewells, not all of them might still be speaking to each other. Perhaps, therefore, it will be just as well to set out the few golden rules of behaviour and suggest ways in which the feminine touch, which is nowadays such a feature of fishing parties, can be turned to advantage in soothing the ruffled egos of mere males – for, when it comes to temperamental behaviour out fishing, it is the male of the species who is by far the worse offender.

On the bigger, grander rivers there is often a situation where there is fishing both from the bank and from a boat. It is generally, rightly or wrongly, considered that the fishermen in the boat, with the benefit of the expertise of the boatman, have the better chance of success. It is, therefore, as bad form to allocate places in the boat unfairly as it is, when placing guns for a pheasant drive, to allocate the best stands for the most important guests. The pecking order on the bank can also be beset with problems.

On all rivers there are certain 'pools' and 'runs' which are better and more likely to hold fish than others and this is perhaps more true of some of the highly-prized trout streams in the south of England where fishable water tends to be in shorter supply.

Where, as is frequently the case nowadays, such waters are owned by a club or syndicate who take it year after year and in which places are only available when one of the existing members dies or otherwise renders himself inactive, it is naturally a matter of the first to arrive on the water each day to have the pick of position. The golden rule, however, observed on most properly organized water is that no rod should remain overlong on one favoured pool but should move on to the next to make way for anyone who might be waiting to follow on behind.

On less regimented waters and particularly where members of the same party all arrive together, the placing of the rods is on a much more informal basis but the same basic rules prevail. Most rented waters are subject to a restricted number of rods and designed to give everyone plenty of room. The cardinal sin is for one of the rods who might be moving down quicker than the man in front of him or might simply get fed up with flogging his own pool, to 'leapfrog' in front of the next man and start casting, thus taking up the water which he is going to fish. To start fishing anything under a hundred yards or so in front of another rod is the height of bad manners and clearly a matter over which offence could rightly be taken.

Should a whoop of delight bring to your notice the fact that one of your fellow fishermen has managed to get stuck into a fish, it is excessively bad manners, however jealous you may feel of his or her success, to grind your teeth, turn your back and redouble your efforts to hook a fish yourself. It is polite, particularly if there is no ghillie, to reel in your own line and dash along the bank to see if you can render any assistance whilst at the same time uttering words of admiration and congratulation. It is extremely bad form, except in the case of a very inexperienced fisherman who might appreciate the benefit of your superior knowledge, to offer words of advice, however well-meaning, on how the fish should be played. Such exhortations as 'For God's sake, keep the tip of your rod up', 'Let the damn thing take line if it wants to', or 'You're bloody well going to lose it if you don't take a proper hold!' will not endear you to the intended beneficiary, particularly if the fish gets off in the end anyway.

On those occasions when the day's activities revolve round the fishing hut rather than those alfresco affairs when everyone brings their own picnic which they sneak off and eat in odd corners as and when the spirit moves them, it is customary for everyone to share the food and drink provided, rather after the same fashion and traditions of the shooting lunch.

It has been remarked elsewhere in this book that fishing, unlike shooting, is a sport in which the ladies take part on completely equal terms with the men. This equality of the sexes does not apply, however, when it comes to catering for the creature needs of the party. This is strictly the responsibility of the women folk and it is wise to appoint one of the sex as head girl with an overall responsibility for supplies, even if this is done on a day-to-day basis with the honour falling to each lady in turn on a rota system. There is nothing more maddening than to find that the salt for the boiled eggs has been left behind or that there is no corkscrew for opening the wine, without being able to lay the blame squarely on one person's shoulders.

This is something to which the most careful consideration should be given when plans are being laid for a mixed fishing party unless the members are wealthy enough to employ the services of the equivalent of a chalet maid after the modern fashion on the ski slopes.

Basically a man has quite enough to do in checking everything he has to take with him so as to be fully operational, such is the complexity of his requirements, to have any time to spare worrying about mundane domestic details. Many a man's day has been ruined by discovering that he has left his Boy Scouts' knife behind.

In the home, however, when it comes to serving one's guests the result of a successful day on the river or loch, the domestic responsibility is much more equally divided. No man worth his salt will trust his wife with anything to do with the serving of trout or salmon, other than the actual cooking and then in the case of an untried wife only under the strictest supervision.

The trouble with the inexperienced housewife is that, faced with the cooking of, say, a twenty-pound salmon for the first time she is apt to lose her head and reach for the nearest cookery book, which will most likely be by Mrs Beeton as being the standard authority for the young bride on all things to do with the running of a household. Now, a great expert Mrs Beeton may have been on how to fold a napkin and even on ten ways of using up old candle ends but great cook she was not. In the case, for example, of cooking a salmon she goes in for all that business of so many minutes per pound and then a bit more with the result that generations of her disciples have suffered from one of the great culinary delights of the table being reduced to something which tastes of nothing, except perhaps overcooked, poor quality newsprint.

Here is the correct way of cooking a salmon whatever size it may be:

> Fill a large cooking vessel – and preferably a proper fish kettle – with cold water to which you can add such suitable seasonings as fennel, the odd bay leaf, an onion, chopped-up carrot, a drop or two of wine vinegar and so on. Put in the fish (which will already have been gutted) and make sure that it is completely covered by the water. Bring to the boil and boil for *exactly three minutes only*. Turn off the heat and leave the fish in the water until it is perfectly cold. Remove the skin and serve. Ideally, the most suitable vegetable to accompany cold salmon are very small new potatoes and the only suitable sauce ever devised is *hol-landaise*.

I am not one of those chauvinistic males who like to maintain that men make better cooks than women but, should there be a scintilla of truth in this, it is largely because men have a better way with sauces and *hollandaise* is one for which the temperament of the male is particularly suited. I also take the view that men are the only ones who can be trusted to boil or scramble eggs to perfection, but that is beside the point.

It is a wise woman who gracefully gives way on this. Like anything to do with eggs, the making of *hollandaise* sauce is a time-consuming and finicky business and it can be much improved by the personal touch. Besides which, it keeps him away from the gin whilst she busies herself with her own more mundane chores.

The other department in which the man of the house should be allowed to reign supreme is when it comes to anything smoked – and particularly smoked salmon.

Whilst it is nowadays possible to buy almost any game or fish most excellently smoked from any good provision merchant, when it is something you have shot or caught yourself, it is a matter of pride and satisfaction to find yourself your own personal smoker. By this I do not mean investing in one of the several types of do-it-yourself, home smokers, adequate though they may be, but that you should seek out a craftsman in the art of smoking to whom you can entrust the job of seeing to your needs, rather in the same tradition as a bespoke tailor. There are many firms, both small and large, up and down the country who take great pride in providing a personal service and, of course, there is all the difference in the world between something that is expertly smoked and something that is not. In fact, much the same difference as between a well-cut and a badly-cut suit.

I was once recommended to a smoker whom, it was alleged, was entrusted with the smoking of all the salmon caught by the Queen Mother and, happening to be in the area, I called upon him to discuss the possibility of my also becoming one of his clients. It was immediately apparent that he was indeed the smoker of the Royal fish for, pinned on the wall above his desk were all the Royal cheques in payment for his services. So proud was he of the Royal patronage that he could not bear to cash them! I must say that he proved to be a master of his trade and his whisky-soaked, oak-chip-smoked salmon was in a class of its own and fit for a Queen. Alas my cheques were not treated with the same reverence as Her Majesty's!

What greater pleasure for a man to tell his guests when carving the smoked salmon, 'Ah yes. This is the fifteen-pounder I caught when fishing with old Bimbo Blood-stock last back end. Only fish of the day, ye know. Straight from the sea. Absolutely covered in sea lice . . .' etc., etc., etc., *ad infinitum*.

Yes! Anything to do with smoking salmon is certainly a man's job! Let the women get on with what they know about like boiling the potatoes and making beds – when they are not catching all the fish!

Rather as a postscript on matters relating to fishy enter-tainment, it might be worth commenting on an odd form of snobbery which seems to persist over the use of fish knives and forks. There are some who hold the view that the use of plated knives and forks for eating fish is a deplorable vulgarity. This strange conceit probably has its origins in Victorian times when fish knives and forks first made their appearance and were sniffed at as a modern invention by the *ancien régime*. There was never any suggestion that they were not practical or that steel knives spoiled the flavour.

This was got round in pre-Victorian times by always using two forks when eating fish. This custom lingered on as a form of inverted-snobbery for a number of years and I believe was still preserved in some of our greater country houses into the present century. It has, however, been long since dropped if only for practical reasons which anyone who has tried eating kipper with two forks will readily understand.

As for the less fortunate, the main reason nowadays for not using proper fish knives is that they are far too expensive.

10

Conservation and the Law

*L*egislation with regard to all aspects of the preservation of game has certain special difficulties to
contend with and the conservation of game fish is no
exception.

There are many who feel that all conservation is merely
designed for the protection of vested interests and for
those who have little practical knowledge of ecology.
Coupled, as this so often is, with unreasoning class hatred
this makes their contribution to any debate on the subject
more noisy than valuable.

Freshwater fish are particularly vulnerable to the dep-
redations of man. Acid rain, bank erosion and the erection
of impassable barriers to spawning beds and so on may
be problems of comparatively recent origin but the most
serious threat of all, pollution, is not.

Industrial pollution has been responsible for the virtual,
extinction of the salmon which used to run up the Con-
tinental rivers. Spain and Portugal, France, Denmark,
Holland, Belgium and Germany all had rivers plentiful
with salmon. In fact, until well on into the nineteenth
century, the Rhine was one of the finest of all salmon

rivers. Anthony Netboy (a pseudonym) records in *The Salmon* that, as late as 1885, the sea nets off the coast near Kralingen on the Dutch coast took 69,500 fish weighing an average of 17 pounds one ounce, whilst Frank Buckland, the famous English Inspector of Fisheries and assiduous chronicler who had a museum devoted to Economic Fish culture in South Kensington, writes on one of the Rhine netting stations on the River Maas, which is only one of the three mouths of the Rhine:

> The principal fishing station is at Orange Nassau, about fourteen miles from the sea; the river here is about nine hundred yards in width, and the nets used eight hundred yards long, thirty feet in depth, and the meshes two and a half inches from knot to knot, or nearly ten inches in circumference. This gigantic net is worked by a steamer of twelve horsepower and a windlass driven by two horses on shore; the fish are not at once killed, but kept alive in a well boat, which is towed to Kralingen, three miles from Rotterdam, and there sold alive to merchants. There are five private fishing stations above Rotterdam. The nets are only worked during the ebb tide.

Buckland goes on to report the fish to be in excellent condition and often weighing forty, fifty and even sixty pounds.

Although pollution has not been nearly as widespread in this country as it has been on the Continent, it appears to have taken effect much earlier and particularly on rivers like the Thames. On one summer's day in 1749 it is recorded that over thirty fish were taken below Richmond Bridge and right up to the end of the eighteenth century there were over 400 professional fishermen earning their living on the river. Then it went into sudden decline.

Records kept of the fishery at Boulter's Landing, near Maidenhead, show that between 1794 and 1821 7,346 pounds weight of salmon were taken, with the number falling drastically each year until, in 1821 when the records ceased, only two fish were taken. Until the present encouraging if small revival, no salmon were recorded as being caught on the Thames after 1830.

Perhaps it is even more striking to mention that during the first half of the nineteenth century, one of the finest salmon rivers in the whole country was the Tyne in Northumberland with annual catches far outnumbering its illustrious neighbour, the Tweed! The dramatic decline of its fortunes were not, as is commonly believed, due entirely to pollution. There were two other contributory factors. The first was a dam that was built twenty-three miles upstream at Bywell which completely cut the salmon off from their spawning grounds and the second was the introduction of stake nets off the coast. Then, in 1864, stake nets were declared illegal in England, though not in Scotland – an anomaly which exists to this day. Three years later the dam at Bywell was blown up and despite the sewage which continued to pour into the Tyne, the fishing immediately showed a vast improvement, a catch of 129,100 being recorded in 1872.

In 1867, however, hang nets were introduced in place of the banned stake nets. At first they made little difference to the rod fishing but the number of hang nets rapidly increased until, twenty years later, it was estimated that off Tynemouth there were twenty-five miles of nets on twenty-two miles of coastline. By the end of the century the salmon catch had fallen to 13,000. Eventually, this once great salmon river ceased to be regarded as a salmon river at all.

There is, however, now distinct evidence that a more enlightened approach to the essentially nineteenth-century pollution problems is showing signs of bearing fruit. Both the Thames and the Tyne are seeing a few fresh running salmon again and, although it seems unlikely that they will ever regain their former glory, there seems to be no reason why the improvement should not continue.

The more modern hazards such as acid rain and bank erosion are problems for which nobody seems to have any solution. It is difficult to envisage legislation which can force farmers to revert to less efficient, old-fashioned drainage schemes at the expense of production.

Whatever can be done about acid rain or even the ozone layer and the Amazonian rainforests are outside the scope of this book so let us look at some more domestic matters.

As long ago as 1962 the Hunter Committee was set up to review the law as it related to the preservation and protection of game and it made a number of what most people regarded as extremely sensible and practical recommendations. And that, for all practical purposes, was that. Not a single recommendation made by Lord Hunter has since been acted upon.

Whilst this deplorable inactivity can be put down to the normal apathy with which the recommendations of government committees are traditionally treated by successive governments, it should also be repeated that as a political issue, anything to do with what are generically known as 'blood sports' is an increasingly sensitive area with the electorate. This has recently been made even more acute by the emergence of the 'Greens' as an almost separate political entity or at least representing an issue on which all politicians feel the need to declare where they stand. This is rather the equivalent of asking the old question 'Have you stopped beating your wife yet?' It is difficult to answer simply 'Yes' or 'No'.

To give the EEC its due it took a great step forward when it banned within its membership the deep sea netting of all salmonids which, with the aid of modern radar detection instruments, was accounting for many thousands of tonnes of fish being intercepted before they ever reached these shores. On the other hand, a new threat to fishing stocks has arisen with the inshore poachers operating illegally off our larger estuaries. Unlike the old netsmen with their ponderous 800-yard-long nets whose activities contributed to the demise of the Rhine as a salmon river, the modern poacher is equipped with monofil nets of up to *two miles* in length which can be comfortably stowed on a small boat. Moreover, if authorities manage to cut or confiscate a net it can be easily, quickly and cheaply replaced with another. Although poaching on the riverbank remains a serious problem, its impact on conservation of fishing stocks is dwarfed by comparison with the operations of the sea poachers.

One of the strangest anomalies of the poaching laws as they exist, is that, whereas any person found in possession of, or attempting to sell, game is required to show that it has been legally acquired, no such restriction applies to anyone in possession of a salmon. Whilst a poacher can be arrested if caught in the act of taking a salmon or with the necessary equipment to do so, the moment the fish has been safely removed from the scene of the crime, he is free to do whatever he wishes.

When the great landowners first took steps to combat the poaching of game, they first made it illegal to sell game at all and, as an additional safeguard, decreed that no one under the social rank of Esquire could legally shoot game in the first place. This was later modified so that game could only be shot by taking out a game licence (as opposed to a simple gun licence) which was jolly expensive, for those days, costing £6 and that game could only be sold to a licensed game dealer which latter condition still applies.

Whilst it is scarcely practical to insist that every fisherman should first take out a rod licence, it is surely not totally impactical, in these days when poachers are out for the biggest profits they can make, that dealers in game fish should be licensed and required only to buy legitimately caught fish. As the law stands at the moment, a boat can come ashore and openly put its large catches of salmon on a fast train to London and sell them on the open market.

This equally applies to the even more ruthless poachers who have replaced the old-fashioned spear-armed gangs and use the aforementioned scientific invention, Cymag. It only takes a few drops of this deadly cyanide-derivative poison to kill everything that swims or crawls in that stretch of water on which it is used and, incidentally, render the water 'dead' for a long time afterwards.

By comparison with problems created by the large scale commercial poachers against whom the law seems so powerless or unwilling to act, other aspects of the law as they relate to fishermen seem to be relatively trivial.

There is, for example, no law in Scotland which makes fishing for trout a crime in itself. A person fishing for trout on private water can in fact only be sued for trespass and this, in turn, means serving a summons on a persistent offender whilst in the act of trespassing. The exception is when a water has been stocked with trout at the expense of the owner or owners, as in the case of a fishing club, with no entry or egress for migratory fish. In this case the fish are the legal property of the owner of the water and any unauthorized person taking a fish can be charged with theft. On many rivers where there is a conflict between the salmon fishing rights which are in the exclusive right of the riparian owner and trout fishing, a solution is frequently found as is normal in England, of granting the trout fishing rights to a club. This not only limits the numbers with a right of access but also offers the comforting consideration that members of a club are the best custodians of their own exclusive rights!

The rights of riparian owners are notoriously areas of conflict between neighbours, taking second place only to disputes over boundaries between owners of even the most modest of properties. They are frequently bitterly contested and handed down from generation to generation to be fought at great private expense in the courts.

One of the most recent of such disputes challenged the question of how far the owner of one bank of a river might transgress on the water of the owner of the other bank in the event, as is very often the case especially on the larger rivers, of their not being one and the same person. The litigant in this case had only recently acquired a stretch of one of the larger and more famous salmon rivers and resented the fact that the owner of the opposite bank could, either by wading or in a boat, cast his lures over his side of the water where, he maintained, were the best salmon lies.

In vain his opposite neighbour protested that there had

been an agreement honoured by generations that each should have the right to fish the whole width of the river on alternate days which was an arrangement on many other stretches of the river where a similar situation existed. The case disturbed the dust on the files of many family lawyers with clients in a similar situation and eventually went to appeal, after conflicting decisions for first one side in the dispute and then the other, to the House of Lords where it was decided that the time-honoured gentleman's agreement had been recognized for so long as to have become sustainable at law and the plaintiff retired from the battle a very much poorer if not wiser man.

Perhaps the most important step forward in lobbying for new legislation for the suppression of large scale poaching is for the public to realize that it is inspired for conservation reasons and not merely for the protection of private interests and that there is nothing glamorous about the new-style poachers who are simply dangerous stop-at-nothing criminals.

Which side of a river a fisherman's fly lands is, in this modern world, not now all that important.

11

Some Coarse Thoughts

*A*ny fisherman, however devoted he might be to the arts of game fishing, who ignores totally the delights and skills of fishing for the many varieties of coarse fish is surely not a true fisherman at heart.

It is probably true to say that there are many forms of coarse fishing which require a more delicate touch – fishing for dace is a good example – than even the most skilful of trout fishing techniques. And what trout fisherman would deny that it requires a quicker eye and a sharper reaction to hook a grayling rising to a fly than the most wily of brown trout.

By contrast the coarse fisherman, dedicated as he is to the study of such a vast variety of baits and tackles as well as to the complexities of the many ways of how they can be presented to a fish, may think of the game fisherman as a bit of a hit-or-miss merchant not to say a trifle short in mathematical perception. Devotees of both codes are, however, united in the derision in which they hold those ignorant, not to say churlish, fellows who ascribe their lack of any interest in fishing to the fact that they 'do not have the patience'. Patience is not high on the list of virtues claimed by most fishermen. They are in the game for the excitement of the chase.

That the 'competition fishing' indulged in by so many of the great fraternity of coarse fishermen sometimes results in almost blank days when very few of the competitors catch any fish at all does not mean that they have been bored witless, dozing off over their rods or whiling their time away doing crossword puzzles. Quite the contrary. They are sitting all the while watching tensely for the slightest twitch of the float to indicate the presence of a potential customer, just in the same way as the game fisherman chafes with impatience at every wasted moment when his fly is not in the water.

There was a recent report of an important coarse fishing contest which threatened to prove one of the blankest of blank days. By lunchtime the faces of the contestants were long indeed for none had had even the tiniest of nibbles. And so it continued throughout the afternoon. Then, just before the contest was due to end one of the competitors hooked a fish and landed it safely. It proved to be the only catch of the day and when weighed before being carefully returned to the water as the rules of competition fishing demand, it tipped the scales at just a fraction over an ounce and a half! Can anyone doubt that the thrill of hooking that minnow proved as great to the outright winner as if he had landed a leviathan!

Then, of course, although it does not come within the scope of this book, there are the varied excitements of sea fishing. Fortunes are paid by the very rich to indulge in big game fishing for such giants of the deep as tunny, barracuda and manta ray (otherwise known as sea vampire) but getting in amongst a shoal of mackerel whilst bobbing about in a small boat with a hand line and a few hooks dressed with a wisp of feather can prove fast and furious fun. As a small boy living in the Orkney Islands, an old man, whom I numbered amongst my greatest friends, used to take me fishing in his tiny boat. One day he hooked a giant conger eel which, after a titanic struggle, he finally managed to haul aboard. It thrashed around alarmingly in the bottom of the boat, barking like a dog as big conger do when they are very angry. Finally, as the old man was trying to extract the hook from its jaws, it reared up and bit the end off his nose before plunging overboard and making good its escape. Even hooking a monster salmon on the Tay can't match that sort of thing for excitement.

Casting aside all prejudice I would say that perhaps the most exciting of all freshwater fish to catch is a monster pike. The current British record for a pike stands at a mere 44 pounds 14 ounces but there is much authenticated evidence of much larger fish being taken than that. For many years the skeleton of a seventy-two pound fish taken from Loch Ken in Galloway was on display at Kenmure Castle but the daddy of them all was found dead in Meelick weir on the River Shannon in Ireland in 1926. This measured sixty-nine inches (one and three quarter metres) in length and a scientist of the Fisheries Department in Dublin estimated its weight as 102 pounds.

Pike are the most voracious and ferocious of our inland fish. Tales of their ferocity abound. Quite recently a lady claimed that a pike had attacked her pet dog when swimming in a lake and had chewed off three of its legs before she had been able to rescue it. I myself once saw, whilst watching a mallard duck leading its baby ducklings in line ahead, a small pike snap up three of them in quick succession before I could chuck a large stone which sent them scuttering to the safety of some nearby rushes. Tales of huge and hungry pike are legion and I am sure no more exaggerated than good fishing stories about any other fish. The excitement of hooking a big 'un and its outstanding courage as a fighter are, however, hard to exaggerate.

When one really gets down to it, perhaps there is more to this Brotherhood of the Angle than one might think.

12

Counting the Cost

O ver the last ten years, fishing has suffered pro-
portionately more severely from rising prices than
any other field sport. Why this should be is not altogether
clear. It is true that, as with shooting, the amount of first-
class fishing available for letting before the last war was
far in excess of demand. Tenants to take beats on a good
salmon river on the long term, were eagerly sought after
and today's practice of letting top-class fishing by the
week or even the day was almost unheard of.

'I hear Rumpty has managed to let his fishing this
season.'

'Lucky chap. Perhaps now he will be able to pay his
tailor's bill,' were the sort of snatches of conversation to
be heard in the smoking room of many a gentleman's
club.

Today the boot is very much on the other foot.
Whereas, in bygone days, the market was dominated by
largely American visitors who probably took the shooting
as well, today the clamorous and ever increasing demand
to rent fishing, and particularly salmon fishing, in the
short term is primarily from the ranks of members of our

own affluent society. Members of the professional classes, like doctors and dentists, manufacturers and property dealers as well as business men who do mysterious things with money in the City, are queuing for a week on a top salmon beat and, in the case of some of the better known, there are lists of names waiting for someone to fall out and a vacancy occur.

Lower down the financial scale, the huge number of trout fishing enthusiasts living in large cities are finding it not only increasingly expensive on the fast developing 'put-and-take' reservoir type fishings, despite the great increase in the amount of water becoming available, but difficult to get a boat without booking well in advance.

At the same time, where the cost of driving a pheasant over the guns at a covert shoot has escalated out of all recognition with the heavy increases in rearing costs, hiring of beaters and many other factors, the man who lets a salmon beat has not suffered in the same way. The salmon which run up his river cost exactly the same as they have always cost – nothing! One can only suppose that it is simply a matter of supply and demand with so many in the market for not enough available water.

One of the additional attractions of fishing as a field sport is that, by comparison with say shooting or hunting, the initial cost of getting kitted out is very much lower. A rod is very much cheaper than a gun and you do not need to buy a horse.

Another consideration for anyone taking up fishing is that it is not something that needs a great deal of training. A man coming new to hunting can make a fearful ass of himself if, when he mounts his horse to partake of the stirrup cup at the beginning of a meet, he falls off the other side. Especially with all those grand folk in their red coats looking on. Similarly, the untrained shot can put his fellow guns and beaters alike in grave danger whilst being the cause of little anxiety to the pheasants or the grouse or whatever else he may be supposed to be aiming at.

So far as the beginner on the river back is concerned, the worst that can befall is that he gets his fishing fly stuck in his own ear and that will be a matter of no consequence to anyone but himself.

The cost of fishing, of course, depends very largely not only on the reputation of the river but the time of the year. There are some rivers which have the reputation for being at their best and providing more fish in the spring whilst others have the reputation for being autumn rivers – 'back-end' fishing as it is called.

It is, therefore, wise for the intending tenant, be it on a daily, weekly, or even longer, basis to know what he is paying for before he puts down his money. An added complication is that many rivers, due to factors which are not always clear, are undergoing drastic changes in their nature; for instance a river once well-known as a spring river, quite suddenly having a much bigger run of autumn fish. This can be due to natural or artificial causes.

A good example of this is the Tay, the largest and some say the best salmon river in Scotland. Its reputation as a spring river once stood supreme. Now it is first and foremost an autumn river. This is obviously reflected in the price a rod would have to pay for a day. The cost of the best stretches of the Tay, which now belongs to the Ballathie House Hotel, gives an indication of how much the changing nature of a river affects what a rod would be likely to have to pay. In the spring an hotel guest can fish for as little as £180 for a week which includes the services of a ghillie and the use of a boat. Later in the year the price for the same facilities will have escalated to £150 per rod *per day*. On other pools, like Islamouth, half a mile upstream, the cost could be as high as £200 a day or more.

Only certain stretches of the famous Border river, the Tweed, command prices of this order, like the Floors Castle beat owned by the Duke of Roxburgh. At Junction Pool, near Coldstream, however, at the height of the autumn run, they charge £3,000 per rod per week! This must surely make it the most expensive fishing water in the world.

The general rule, when it comes to salmon fishing, is that the further north, the lower the cost. The exception is the majestic Dee, in Aberdeenshire, which, with its Royal Deeside connections, is both one of the most expensive and the most exclusive of all the salmon rivers.

The more northerly rivers are what are known as 'spate' rivers. That is to say that they are hill rivers which are liable to sharp fluctuations in the amount of water coming down. One moment the water level can be so low that you can wade across them, and the next a rainstorm in the hills can turn them into a raging torrent. To a degree this makes them more of a gamble for the fisherman who may have the bad luck to hit a patch when there is not enough water for the fish to run up and, as he will certainly be assured, they are all splashing around in their thousands off the river mouth waiting for the next flood. On the other hand, should the water be just right, the spate rivers can provide the best of sport.

Of these rivers, the Spey, which flows northwards into the Moray Firth, is the largest and the best with some famous beats like Castle Grant and Cairnton with a rod costing upwards of £100 a day. A first-class beat on the Spey for a *party of six rods*, at the height of the season, costs anything between £1,500 and £3,000 a week. This puts it in range as a river that is practical for a party of friends to take for a week or longer and share the costs. Indeed so many do, year after year, that it is not easy to get on to the best beats without going on a waiting list.

The same applies, except more so, on those several excellent small rivers in Invernesshire like the Oykel, the Helmsdale or the Brora which are even less expensive and, in consequence, much in favour with the younger set who like to make up parties of their own age and inclinations.

With these sort of prices being readily paid for fishing, it is not suprising that, on those rare occasions when the freehold of one of the better beats comes into the market, it enters the realms of very big business indeed. When, some eight years ago, a private individual paid a sum in excess of £2 million for one of the best beats on the Tay, it was the general consensus of local opinion that he had taken leave of his senses. Today multi-million pound bids for the best fishings are commonplace.

A comparatively new development in this world of high finance is the selling of the freehold of a fishing on a time-share basis, although the imagination boggles at the prospect of investing in the same week on a salmon beat, in sickness or in health, year in and year out, in perpetuity. On a more modest financial level, another comparatively new development in the financial structure of the salmon fishing world may be worth commenting on. This is the advent of the salmon farm.

The rearing of salmon in captivity – in large free-floating 'cages' – from fry to ready-for-the-table, has escalated prodigiously over the last few years. It is now estimated that there are twenty-five times more farmed salmon than wild fish in Scottish waters and this has brought with it all manner of unforeseen problems. Not the least of these is that it has resulted in the price of salmon falling dramatically.

Before farm-reared salmon started to flood the market – and before the vast rise in the price of fishing – it was not altogether unknown for a lucky fishing tenant with a large catch to be able to recoup at least a considerable part of his rental by selling his fish. Today the salmon farms are so over-producing that they are lucky if they can sell their fish for much over £2.50 a pound. This, together with other problems like escaping fish, is threatening to put some of the less efficient producers out of business. There is also a very real danger of released or escaped farm-bred salmon seriously endangering stocks of wild fish for they cannot exist harmoniously with each other. None of which is very good news for the fishing tenant.

Although this survey of the financial implications of joining the fishing set is largely concerned with salmon fishing in Scotland, it does more or less exactly reflect the general escalation of prices for both salmon and trout fishing throughout the country. In England the amount of *Lebensraum* is even more restricted so that practically all the water on splendid trout and salmon rivers like the Test are now totally owned in the long term by clubs or syndicates making access for the outsider almost impossible.

At the same time there are still, here and there, rivers and lochs where the fisherman can enjoy wonderful sport at wonderfully low prices. There are still, in more remote regions, rivers where sport can be enjoyed for the modest price of a day's ticket and sometimes, even, for the courtesy of asking. For the dedicated fisherman, not too much concerned with social cachet, the outlook is perhaps not so intimidating as the figures quoted here might suggest. Long may it stay that way.